Happy Birthday
James.!

love always
Emma Jane
xxx

24/04
2012

No gears, no brakes. Just a frame, two wheels,
handlebars, and some cranks.

When I ride my bike I am in the world. When I drive my car I am as disconnected as if I were watching someone else play Mario Kart. I don't want to hide from the world. I'll take life, with all its risk and immediacy, over comfort any day.

Front Cover Photo: Tristan Wheelock

First published in Great Britain in 2010 by Pro-actif Communications
Livingstone House, 29 High Northgate, Darlington, Co. Durham DL1 1UQ
www.pro-actif.co.uk
email: sales@pro-actif.co.uk

© Pro-actif Communications
www.42x12fixed.co.uk

Written by: Patrick Potter

Printed on natural recyclable products (ie paper).
Printed in China.

ISBN: 978-0-9559121-3-9

Carpet Bombing
Culture
Since 2007

# 42 x
# 12

The Cult of Fixed

Published by Pro-actif. Written by Patrick Potter

Think of bicycles as
rideable art that can just
about save the world.

Grant Petersen

Just who is the Fixie rider?

## The Myth of the Fixie Rider

Who is the Fixie rider? It's a buzz question now that a lot of people will want to know for both nefarious reasons and benign. If we are to believe the less than kind internet banter on the topic then the Fixie rider is a horribly spoilt late twenty something male of affluent background, who has never been required to grow up and who spends all his pocket money on cool toys and fads in a never ending effort to be trendy. Cynics would say that the Fixie rider is a myth in the process of being invented by those people who want to sell stuff to rich kids; the brands.

Let's loosen up a little because life's just too short to be that cynical. Let's assume that people ride Fixed gear because it's fun. Then surely we are nearer the mark when we assert that the real Fixie rider is someone who likes bicycles and also likes having fun. If this is true then we can deduce that the Fixie rider ain't just riding Fixies.

A quick look around the scene will reveal that most people who like bikes, like bikes. Some say they went to Fixies from BMX looking for a way to get a little older, a little more gracefully. Some just had to try it out for the craíc. Whatever the route, a lot of existing riders just chucked their Fixie in the garage alongside the road bike, BMX, mountain bike, classic roadster and tandem.

As for those young people who are as venal and banal as to want to be urgh 'cool'. They have come to bicycles with an impure heart and should be struck down by Thor's hammer for their impertinence. Alternatively they could just be having fun too. Who knows, maybe they'll try other bikes too? Fixie culture has often been cited as a 'Gateway drug' into harder and harder stuff.

This raises some interesting questions in itself. If Fixed Wheel is smoking weed then what is the cycling equivalent of heroin or crack cocaine? Magic mushrooms = Penny Farthing?

The bottom line is that only two types of people really need to have a 'fixed' (sorry) idea of who the fixed wheel rider really is. They are: Marketers and Haters. The rest of us can quite happily exist in a state of grace where identity itself is a pretty interplay of shadows and light, a game to while away the time, rather than another useless dogma.

Amen.

So who is the fixie rider?

Sometimes it's better not to know . . .

## Hamlet is my homeboy

To ride or not to ride? Is it nobler in the mind to ignore everything else you have to do and just spend the whole day on the bike, or get everything done now so you can get more time on the bike later? That is the question. For who could be bothered to go to the supermarket or pay the bills at the post office were it not for the threat of something after, some sort of punishment like having to eat cold pasta whilst hiding from the rent collector?

RIDE BACKWARDS! (The Freedom of Limitation)

## RIDE BACKWARDS! (The Freedom of Limitation)

More freedom is equal to less limitation right? Wrong! Total freedom is a meaningless void of choice without consequence and therefore without effect. Real freedom is the freedom to choose your limitations? Wrong again! We don't choose the limitations of physical reality. How we respond to those limitations is however, within our control and therefore that is a kind of freedom. So freedom is a relative phenomenon that exists in relation to our limitations. Freedom is riding backwards.

When you ride fixed gear you lose one rather important freedom, the freedom to stop pedalling. You lose, arguably less important choices including which of your 21 gears will best suit the hill ahead of you. Finally, if you're hardcore, you also lose the freedom to decelerate rapidly by applying brake blocks to the rim of your bike wheels using a lever on your handlebars.

Why cast away these choices? Why would anyone choose to actually increase their limitations?

The first answer is simple. To cast aside one freedom is often to discover another 'new' freedom that was hidden by the old mindset. Freedom is riding backwards. You can't ride backwards on a freewheel set-up.

The second answer is potentially 'deeper'. By removing technological 'advantages' from our relationship with the physical world we force the body and the mind to compensate. This compensation activates reserves of capacity in the individual and the re-discovery of these capacities is enormously exciting.

The drive of technology has always been towards reducing the amount of effort we have to use to achieve any goal. We are perhaps now, just beginning to realise that certain skills and talents that we have as human beings are atrophying as a result.

Maybe now it's time to take back some of our freedom to experience limitation. It's exciting that people are starting to think in terms of creating value by removing pre-supposed material advantages. Put simply, it's subversive to have more fun by needing less.

Of course nobody is saying that Fixie culture is deliberately operating on such a philosophical level. It's just that the urge towards freedom as expressed in this tendency is exciting because it's topsy-turvy. And that playful topsy-turviness is perhaps something of wider significance.

Until very recently, western culture has always supposed that the mind is stimulated by intellectual pursuits and the body by sports. This separation is false of course. The mind is just as involved in riding backwards as it is in any quadratic equation. And ultimately it's in the mind that the joy of riding a bike is experienced. Feeling free is something that happens to the whole self, body and mind included.

Freedom is a fleeting experience that can be found and re-found in many different ways. Almost always it has to be approached playfully. Play is a very serious matter. A wise man once said that 'freedom is just the opportunity to be better.'

Stay playful! Keep riding backwards!

It's not so much to me about coolness factor as it is about feeling. Not that 'zen' feeling either. Whoever first coined that shit is retarded. It more about the feeling of sheer terror that rushes through you when you're hauling ass at a yellow light that's just turned red. That or rolling down a really steep hill and keeping it under control. It's more of a 'holy shit I made it without dieing' thing . . .

Alan Sikiric, NYC

# Frame Wars
# Episode I: Steel is real

The frame wars have raged ever since some bright spark realised that aluminium could reduce frame weight and theoretically give riders an edge in professional racing. Whether or not the weight advantage actually is an advantage at all should be a question reserved for roadies and their team mechanics.

Regardless of what the pro-racer needs, aluminium then titanium and now carbon-fibre are all hot products in the consumer cycling market and the professionals are paid great sums to ride certain frames to ensure that the man in the street will spend serious money on exotic materials.

So what, for the uninitiated reader, constitutes the basic argument between traditional welded steel frames and the new pretenders to steel's throne?

Ok, let's throw our hat in the ring. Basically: invest in steel. Unless you're a pro racer, the weight advantage of any other material is not proportionate to the additional cost or the potential concomitant shortened lifespan found in urban riding. There are many ways to get faster (do fries go with that shake?) and reducing the weight of your bicycle frame is one of the least effective or efficient.

But what of Carbon Fibre? Basically, it's still early days and therein lies it's problem. There's really no heritage to speak of. It's just plain difficult to get excited about a composite laminate. There's no legacy, little narrative and it's unlikely to be getting intimate with the adjective 'classic' anytime soon. Although the technology of carbon is proven, the steel frame has the advantage of having been developed continuously over a long period of time by the many shining minds applied to bicycle engineering. Carbon Fibre is still just a baby in comparison. Those that argue that Carbon Fibre offers a wider range of frame designs are overlooking the fact that the existing diamond shape is the product of generations of evolution and is damn near perfect for purpose.

So there you are. The latest generation of steel frames are lighter thanks to the thinner tube walls made possible by the material's strength. The weight difference ain't what it was twenty years ago. And ultimately we don't want to have to buy a new bike every year, do we?

Full Flow

**Full Flow - Keirin**

The lurid colours of the Keirin line-up are reminiscent of a bag of sweets. Or perhaps better said, they're the image of a greyhound race and that's not so far from the truth. The neon rainbow of lycra on display helps to differentiate the riders for the guys in the tote shops, watching the races on TV sets, clutching their betting slips. The Keirin race evolved as a gambler's sport. Vast sums of money change hands over the races in Japan and the S Class riders are superstars.

Riders are classed by their type of strength. Those with great endurance are called 'Senko' riders and those with a powerful but short sprint are known as 'Oikomi'. The excitement for the spectator lies in

trying to predict how riders will co-operate by forming lines as a winning strategy. Riders will even state in advance of the race what line they plan to form.

The amount of money involved in Keirin puts a lot of pressure on the sport making it very highly regulated. Failed races can cost millions of yen. The bicycles used must be approved and the parts are largely identical, leaving the race to be determined by the guts, brawn and wit of the riders. It's grindingly physical racing. The school of Keirin trains its racers fifteen hours a day. The races themselves get up to seventy kilometres an hour. Crashes happen.

As the 'Japanese Keirin Association' proudly asserts, "The powerful races all driven by a rider's power are similar to martial arts."

To re-iterate, these guys are tough.

Keirin is of course no longer a secret of the orient and the culture of Keirin is influential and in no small way – really cool. Pretty much everything Japanese is cool simply by virtue of being Japanese and Keirin is doubly so for western cycling devotees. The flavour of the sport is wasabi like in its intensity, and just that little bit edgier than European-style track racing. These factors combine to give Keirin an attractive aura for new fans of riding.

The theatricality of a Kierin race is unsurpassed. The slow steady build up as the nine riders fall into place behind the pacer is soon followed by the incredible increase of speed as a manic gong sounds to indicate that the race is in full flow. The fleeting moments of hustle between the competing lines seem to take place in a moment of suspended time. Finally, at the finish line fortunes are won and lost.

You pays your money, you takes your chances.

## Old dog, new tricks?

There are those who are openly hostile to the idea of doing tricks on a Fixie. And yet, with the advent of purpose built Trick-Track-Street bikes it seems clear that the sport is both here to stay and set to grow. There are two driving factors in this development. One is that the BMX generation has grown up. The other is that the new breed of road bike is simply more useful in general, bridging a gap between a tool for urban transportation and a toy for urban play. A rider can see an opportunity for a nice little jump and instead of riding home to switch bikes they can simply do it 'en route'.

Although it is currently clear from the spate of videos online that the Fixie is nowhere near as versatile for tricks as the trusty BMX, there is still a lot of boundary breaking going on and some individuals, such as Tom LaMarche and John Prolly, are really pushing it forward. So it is that once again what Fixie offers the rider is the opportunity to break new ground. You would have to turn invisible or internally combust mid-trick to do something new on a BMX. On a Fixie you could still be the first man or woman to pull a new stunt. There's a move out there just waiting for you to put your name on it.

Incidentally, you may or may not be aware that Fixed Wheel tricks are as old as the hills. Well back in 1899 all bicycles were fixed gear so it wasn't perhaps as much of a statement. They even made videos for Youtube, which was incredibly far-sighted if you consider that Youtube wasn't to be invented for another 100 years. Yet more evidence that it's all been done before. Oh well.

## Messengers: "Your career is in my bag - how much is it worth?"

The rock stars of the business world, picking and dropping anything and everything and looking good doing it. Big dictators of street fashion, with a following of a thousand hipsters.

The fastest moving objects on a city block, hot knifing through the butter, surfing lights and straightening lines. Where good days are measured by the "flow" - when everything's clockwork: weather, dispatcher, work, the bike, lock-down, lifts, clients, pedestrians, jock-cops, mounting, the ride and uninterrupted shaping of traffic.

Going breakneck but still being the controller, a calculated complex equation resulting in the buzz of being one, being fast, being smooth and getting away with it.

Topping out on the cycling evolutionary scale, each task meticulously honed to subconscious efficiency, culminating into a well-oiled mile-eating, pedal churning delivery machine.

Exterior - a tight knit work-hard play-hard underground city sub-cell that acceptance to can only be earned by blood, sweat and toil from the road.

Interior - some of the most honest, unpretentious, fun, friendly "I got your back jack", well educated, creative people you will ever meet.

The bad days sometimes show, they will *always* be bitchy, if anything gets in and breaks the "flow".

*Khaled Ben-Rabha*

Moving Meditation

## Moving Meditation

Things have a habit of returning from the archives of history, called forth by new acolytes to adorn themselves in new forms. Rolling forth from the velodromes of Europe where the gods of continental cycling feast on the joy of motion, track bikes came. Tearing up the metropolises of New York, Tokyo, SF and London new knights on steel steeds are it's disciples.

A new breed of track bike rider was forged then. Riders trapped between the necessities of riding cheap, tough and simple-to-fix bikes and the heady joy of heightened awareness that comes from having neither adequate braking nor an ability to coast. A strange breed of men then, whose insistence on ripping the arse out of life would not sit well with the sedentary office jobs of their peers.

The fixed-wheel, fixed-gear or simply 'Fixie' bicycle has, for better or worse, become the focus of a sub culture all of its very own.

There are those who come to Fixies from the manly and serious world of road racing citing the bicycles considerable capacity to strengthen the legs and improve 'souplesse'. There are those who come simply because it's fantastic fun to learn the new awareness and co-ordination required to make Fixies fly. Then are those who come because it's really, really cool and the bikes are well, sweet. And finally there are those who come by mistake and leave shortly afterwards.

All these pilgrims are rewarded. For it was written long ago that they would come. And above all the Fixie offers a new perspective on riding a bicycle. And it is a perspective that many claim to be a gateway to a mysterious 'zone' wherein the body and cycle become one with the road, time compacts and the mind is for a few priceless moments chained to the moment in all its ragged glory.

In short, it is a moving meditation.

## Devil take the hindmost

The plans for the first known bicycle were originally handed to the mage Dr. Faust in the middle ages. Faust arranged for the machine to be built for him by track demons as part of an attractive package of benefits given to him on contract (buy now pay forever) with the angel of the morning (AKA Satan). Even now it is said that if you should encounter Satan and he be in the mood for dragging you to the deepest pits of Sheol for an eternal duration of torture (SATC Marathon), all you have to do is challenge him to a track race. Satan is obliged by the demonic code to agree and of course his hands are far too big and gnarly to hold the Cro-Mo track bars, and if that isn't advantage enough just think of all the extra drag his wings and horns are going to bring to the table. Problem solved.

## A Fixie Soap Opera

No doubt being whispered about in the hallowed corridors of television production as we speak: the Fixie Soap Opera. Sound far-fetched? Think again, if you were lucky enough to catch a few episodes of 'Pacific Blue' you'll know what I mean. Cops on bicycles chasing criminals plastered in orange fake tan and sporting an extra-terrestrial line in botoxed facial features, that's right - it was set in California. But so what? Surely this does not precipitate the existence of a Fixie 90210?

Of course it does, it's just a matter of time. It only remains for us to try and catch a glimpse of the beast, maybe even write ourselves into a job down at the network.

Where would the show be set? - In San Francisco of course. Those steeps are such a gift to a DOP with a bent for dramatic establishing shots. Opening credits roll with a not-too-rough-pop-punk-melody and a medley of riders bombing traffic then waving and smiling at the audience in an 'Oh hey! Glad you dropped by' kind of way. The viewer is immediately hooked.

And what of the characters?

Well as television execs know, poor people make for bad TV so let's centre the show around a phenomenally wealthy couple a la 'The OC' yet somehow retain an edgy vibe by inventing a vaguely criminal history for their son/nephew/whatever who has come to live with them and is of course the real star. Match him up with a kooky twat to act as a 'Chandleresque' comedic foil and hey presto we have a show. Now all we need is an array of milky bland shiny haired female sops to ponce about being indecisive about who they want to sleep with. Mix it all up with a couriers versus hipsters theme, some stunts and a little of that MASH style action and it'll run for years. You heard it here first people. Now go! Make it happen!

Zen & The Art of
Bicycle Maintenance

### Zen & the Art of Bicycle Maintenance

Let's see if we can split you and your friends up into two definitive camps. (The following is based on the theories of Mr. Robert M. Pirsig.)

Read the following two texts and decide which describes you best.

## Option A

When you think about cycling you just want to get up and get on a bike and mess around. You would often be equally happy spending the afternoon tinkering with a pile of frames, spindles, cranks, sprockets, chains and pedals. If you catch a comment on a blog about anything you disagree with you have to respond. You have a workshop space. You don't buy bikes you buy bike components. You can't ride something without altering it. You feel very proud of yourself when you improvise parts, alter parts to fit frames they shouldn't or even make bits from scratch. You understand the engineering principles underlying the concept of a bike. You are never too fussy about making the final rig look pretty.

## Option B

You love to ride just as much as Mr A. However, you also love to be seen riding and your bike is absolutely beautiful. When you speak names like Mercian and Campagnolo you do so in a hushed and reverent whisper. You would consider buying a beautiful bicycle even if you knew the set up was less than suitable for you. You would somehow convince yourself that you could wear it in. When it comes to modding the aesthetics of your machine you are all over it, but you'd rather have a pro do the paint work. You don't own more than the most basic tools and re-fitting the chain is about the limit of your repair capacity. It's not that you couldn't fix it yourself, you're bright enough but it just doesn't feel right. You want the job done properly. The idea of using non-proprietary parts to fix your machine is vaguely disgusting to you.

**If you find yourself in camp A then you are what Pirsig called a CLASSICIST.**

A Classicist is focused on the reality of underlying form (Like the man himself.) A classicist finds beauty in the harmony of logic. A classicist is often called a 'Geek'. The classicist knows that the reality of a bike is actually the idea of a bike and the physical bike is just a manifestation of that idea. Function excites the classicist. Fitness for purpose, and efficiency and the power of applied thinking all excite the classicist. Looking pretty is viewed as a shallow concern by the Classicist. He or She is less aware of surface appearances and not very interested in glamour or illusion. The classicist understands that they have to kind of look decent but the act of dressing themselves does not excite them. As a result they will often dress neutrally. They are not necessarily tidy people, but they do know exactly where everything is. At the party, they are the ones in the kitchen earnestly discussing things. They like giving directions.

**If you find yourself in camp B then you are, by Pirsig's definition a ROMANTIC**

The Romantic is focused on the dazzling reality of surface appearances. Greatly moved by visual beauty and equally disturbed by visual ugliness the Romantic is an emotional creature. Believing that emotional reactions are the root of an authentic experience of life the Romantic will not tolerate his or her experiences to be analysed and dissected. A Romantic is often called a 'Hipster', a 'Hippy' or a 'Pretentious Twat'. Beauty excites the Romantic, as much in the beauty of ideas as the beauty of colour and light. The Romantic will often daydream about cycling. It will be a daydream full of sunshine and great feelings of joy. Romantics can also become enamoured of darker feelings and go for a walk on the more 'Goth/Emo' side. Romantics are very occupied by the current moment or phase and feel very sincerely involved with things that they will quite soon after forget about in favour of something new. The lure of the new is very strong for the Romantic. At the party the Romantic is trying to either make everybody laugh or fancy them. If you ask them for directions they will smile and wave a hand in a vague direction.

Pirsig reckons that this division is total, meaning that everybody is on one side of the line or the other and that neither side can really appreciate the other. Evidence is in abundance to suggest that this war between two tribes really does exist in our culture. Look for example at all the bloggers pouring vitriolic scorn on the new scene-kids being attracted to Fixie culture by the pretty 'colorways' and messenger chic. What is that if not the rage of Classicist against Romantic?

So the big question remains... Can the Romantic and the Classicist ever be friends?

Yes of course! Who is going to fix the Romantic's bike? Who is going to give the Classicist a make-over? That's right people. It's time to bury the hatchet and declare peace. Both world views are equally valid. Let's come together through cycling.

Peace.

Don't ride to live; live to ride.

## Re-inventing the wheel

Spokes are fantastic for doing their job and furthermore they make great spoke card holders or more importantly, you can put those things on that used to come free in cereal boxes. What were they called? Anyway they made a hell of annoying sound so they went out of style pretty fast. Or are they back 'in' now? Let me know.

Now what's hot is having at least one wheel with those fancy flat three spoke type arrangements. What are they called? Anyway, they do look fly but they sure are expensive. Well everything is expensive these days, have you seen the price of milk? Where are these kids getting their money from?

She ain't nothing but a goldsprinter

### She ain't nothing but a goldsprinter

In Post WW2 Britain, when a chap wanted to take his mind off the horrors of the recent past and the deprivation of the present, he went down the Music Hall. These venerable old institutions provided variety shows of the sort still seen at the more traditional British Holiday Camps. Well, except that music hall was a little bit saucier in an innocent 'Carry On' kind of way. Comedians with ludicrous catchphrases, singing, dancing and bizarre musical instruments were all employed to raise the spirits of the audience. And, of course there was roller racing . . .

During the interval of the main show, bicycles rigged up to rollers were brought on. These early devices were mechanical and a belt powered by the rollers drove the mechanism of a large clock so that the audience could see who was winning. The winner was the first cyclist to do roughly half a mile.

The culture of roller racing peaked in the fifties with British legend Eddie Wingrave touring the country challenging all-comers to take him on in front of huge audiences. At times the number of challengers was so great that the stage hands threatened to strike. All of the Mecca dancehalls (Now Bingo halls)

possessed roller racing rigs. As Wingrave notes in the mini-documentary on the history of the sport produced by the ubiquitous Buffalo Bill, 'you couldn't tell who was going to be good at it, it wasn't always the best road racers who won.'

Roller racing dropped out of fashion (along with music hall) in the UK presumably as a consequence of the golden age of cinema dawning and subsequently, television. It wasn't until the 1990's that it began to make a comeback in Europe, rebranded as 'Goldsprinting'. The sport was revived by a Swiss Velophile and brewery owner, thus establishing the strong link between beer and roller racing that exists today.

It just so happened that the 1999 CMWC took place in Zurich and naturally the hosts laid on Goldsprints as part of the tournament. Messengers from around the world were introduced to the game, including Caspar Hughes and Paul 'Winston' Churchill from London. Hughes and Churchill were immediately captivated by the insane energy of the roller race and determined to bring it back to the UK in a big way. And so it was that Rollapaluza came to be.

The current incarnation of the sport is fierce, fun and informal. Much like the original it is an inclusive sport inviting anyone who feels lucky to have a go.

Above all it's the atmosphere that makes it such a hit. In the back rooms of bars, drunken fans woop and holler like packs of coyotes while two racers frantically sweat and grimace their way through the most intense thirty seconds you can have with your clothes on. Loud and dirty music (often live) whips up the onlookers into an increasingly bestial frenzy. It's intimate, face to face action; you can literally smell the sweat and feel the burn.

Just don't mention the words 'lactic acid'.

It's harder than a bag of hard things. My heart is in my mouth, my lungs are like crisp bags and it feels like I'm breathing through a straw. My legs on the other hand? It feels like someone's doused them in petrol and set them alight.

## The Shangri-la rig

The stark, stripped down and gleaming, white bicycle hung, shining like an angel in a nativity play, in the window of the bike shop. It whispered gently, a song on the edge of perception. If one could have made out the words from the glistening breath of soundless sounds she made, it might have been the words of an exquisite poem told about golden days on silver highways. She sings of utopia, just you and your beautiful machine, with all those you pass struck dumb in awe at your grace, at your velocity, at your union. You must have it, you must have this bicycle regardless of the cost and yet when you reach out to caress the pearlescent paint it disappears, for it is the 'Midas Fixie', the machine of legend that can never be touched...

No chain. AKA. Putting the hammer down.

## Hit the road Jack

Cyclists are not foppish intellectuals; they are men and women of action. Consider if you will the average fixed gear or general cycling blog. Heavy on the words? No indeed. These velo warriors do not have time to wax lyrical in such a paltry medium. The internet is for them a source of bicycle porn, pictures of beautiful components and a YouTube gateway to NYC Bike Messengers on crack. And this is as it should be.

There are some exceptions to this rule. Bike Snob NYC, Urban Velo and Moving Target Zine are all rivetting reads with some fine and thoughtful or just plain funny writing going on. Check it.

And yet, who has time to sit around typing when we could just as happily express what we mean to say with the video camera on our iPod nano, out in the streets, cycling like men! In fact, what are you doing here, sat in your smoking jacket and plus fours in your town house reading room while the Moroccan house boy prepares a tagine of five spice lamb and dose of opium? Get your cut off Dickies on man! Pump up them tyres and telephone your homeboys!

We are not readers! We are men and women of action!

## The Secret Joy of Bleeding

Secretly we all long to die. No hang on, that's not quite right. Or is it? But anyway, the question that I've been meaning to ask is this: isn't there a secret joy to coming off the bike? Think back to the hurly burly of childhood. Conjure up a vision of those wild days careering up and down the street with your little pack of neighbourhood chums on your bikes and scooters and roller skates and whatever other wheeled contraption you got last birthday.

Now remember those timeless moments of horror as you suddenly realised that a fierce collision with concrete was now inevitable. (About three times a week I seem to recall) Do you remember the dizzy vertigo of that split second before impact? Do you remember the dull thud and the dizzy high of mild concussion? Can you picture the glistening rivulets of scarlet suddenly trickle forth from the new wounds? Wasn't it secretly brilliant!? Then there was the heroic trek home like a war veteran coming in to receive glory and fuss from mum and dad.

And now when you're out there trying out how many tricks you can still do from your BMX days on your Fixie, in short 'growing up' disgracefully, isn't there are part of you that is still motivated by the secret joy of bleeding?

I still feel that variable gears are only for people over forty-five.

Isn't it better to triumph by the strength of your muscles than by the artifice of a derailer?

We are getting soft . . .
As for me, give me a fixed gear!

Henri Desgrange, Founder of the Tour de France,
L'Équipe article of 1902

Riding a fixed-gear is like handicapping yourself. The bikes are so awkward to ride that not looking like an idiot while riding one is an accomplishment. It's like riding a three-legged horse in the Kentucky Derby. To do that well, you'd have to be an excellent jockey.

*San Francisco Bay Guardian*

## The Quest for The Holy Grail?

Long have men sought it. It is rumoured that he who possesses it shall have everlasting life and will sit at the right hand side of Eddy Merckx in the mighty halls of Velo-halla. It is known only as 'The Hour Record'. An hour of what? You may cry. An hour of ecstatic agony in which you are brought face to face with all of your demons and all of those demons shall be called 'pain'. Failure is almost guaranteed and yet, here you must come sooner or later to face the race of truth.

In theory the hour record is a simple matter. One man, one track bike, one velodrome and one hour. However, when the difference between breaking and not breaking the record is so tremendously small there is much to quarrel over when it comes to the fine details. The icy glare of the UCI is ever present and their rules are stringent.

Not so very long ago the UCI retrospectively downgraded every hour record holder from 1972 until 2000. Why? Because they were all deemed to have had an unfair equipment advantage over Merckx. Disc wheels, 'praying mantis' style handlebars, chest pads, airfoil tubing, tri-spokes and 'superman' riding positions. The pretenders to the throne must have been devastated as they saw their places in Velo-halla snatched away from them.

In spite of this the UCI still awards 'Best Human Effort' to any rider achieving a record without restricting themselves to the classic bike technology of the early 1970's. (Namely a round-tubed diamond frame with conventionally spoked wheels and drop handlebars.)

Perhaps it is best after all that the UCI Hour Record remains rooted in a 'classic' tradition as it just wouldn't be fair on Eddy to ride it on anything else. So if you do set out to seek the grail my friends, make sure to choose the right steed for the quest, and that may not necessarily mean *the fastest*.

Velorotica

## Velorotica

It was only a matter of time. The innate sexual energy of the 'sport' must bubble forth no matter how decent and god fearing folk might try to deny it. There is something sexy about riding bikes. Perhaps it is the act of riding itself that is so eroticised? To take machine between your legs and subject it to your control to give you power. And then to work so very physically hard with body and soul to imbue said host with all your virile energies while sweating and grunting, while muscles bulge and great cyclist calves ripple with power.

Who knows? But just as all porn tends to start with the female body, Velorotica begins with pretty girls on bikes. And the 'Chicks and Bikes' blog provides exactly that in a gently erotic 'pin up' setting. The Japanese also have their own 'Girls on Bicycles' to showcase the young ladies of Tokyo. These sites alone are not proof of a wave of bike porn (that is to come) but rather evidence of a Fixie orientated lad's magazine culture developing.

The true pioneers of Velorotica are the Portland group 'Bike Smut' who have not only shot several true bike porno movies (Look for "Cycle Bound" – not available on DVD, you have to arrange a screening) they have also arranged a touring bike porn festival. These guys have taken the implied sexuality of cycling and made it a touch more overt. It's also funny and positive too which is something missing from most porn these days. You have to admire the self spanking cycling machine.

If you can't wait for the Bike Porn festival to come to a town near you then you can get a quick fix by watching the Peaches video "Lovertits" in which Peaches indulges in some hardcore Velorotica with a friend proving as ever that's she's an electro punk genius and years ahead of her time.

(Thanks to Ryan Bigge of 'The Bigge Idea' for the lead on the Peaches video)

The call of the mild

### 'The Call of the Mild'

Being a treatise on the rise & rise of anarcho-dandyism and its expression in the form of the 'Tweed Run'

*Chap Magazine*

The underground art school fanzine that started a quiet revolution in the opium dens of fin de siècle (20th siècle) London.

Emerging from the heady milieu of London town at the time of the turn of the millennium, an art school fanzine knows as 'Chap' introduced an intriguing set of ideas on gentlemanly deportment that were at once firmly rooted in a nostalgia for times passed and yet thoroughly suffused with a subtle yet powerfully subversive aroma of revolution.

'Chap magazine' was and continues to be quietly influential. On the surface what appeared to be a thoughtless yet delightful game of nostalgia soon revealed itself to be highly intelligent and wildly amusing satire. 'Chap' was a clever game that offered the reader the chance to play along. To adopt the stance of the 'Anarcho-Dandyist' one would reject the perceived flaws of modern life in a highly elegant manner while simultaneously satirising the world of the 'Dandy' from which one's identity was being borrowed.

For the 'Chap' a comfortable existence driven by an unbridled appetite for pleasure was the goal and if that involved occasionally dabbling in forbidden pleasures such as the opium den, black magic and long afternoons with a pipe in the reading room then so be it.

Elegant subversion did not as one might expect fade away in the manner of a fad. 'Chap' proved to be an attractive lifestyle option for young men rendered listless by the ridiculous prattle of the 'Lad's Mag'. It seems that 'Chap' touched a nerve and found some wider resonation with the 21st century zeitgeist. 'Chap' no longer seems quite so bizarre in the context of current trends in vintage fashion and the increasingly popular steam-punk aesthetic that also has a playfully subversive take on Victoriana.

We can conclude without great hesitation that the efforts of 'Chap' mastermind Gustav Temple laid no small part of the cultural foundation upon which the institution of the London Tweed Cycling Club has now been built. Indeed, Temples' masterly prose style has been very widely borrowed from, both in the TCC's literature and in this very text.

### The 'City' bike and the associated return of the 'Roadster'

Wherein the rising popularity of the commuter bicycle and the associated return to popularity of early twentieth century style bicycles are discussed

The mighty Roadster (perhaps better said; Roadster 'style'.) bicycle has, like the dinosaurs once did, roamed the earth a great deal longer than the pesky titanium and carbon mammals that now take its place. Even now in those exotic areas of the world where the bicycle is still a work horse rather than a play thing, the Roadster style is prevalent. The reason is simple. They are functional and they last forever. These classic machines have acquired a renewed aura of desirability for devotees of the Tweed lifestyle. They have about them the austere beauty of a North Yorkshire autumn and the noble allure of a stately home.

*"Discerning cyclists recognise that bicycle technology reached its pinnacle in the early 1970s and everything since has just been marketing."*

*The Tweed Cycling Club*

Quite. Behind the playful stance there is a real criticism being made here. Adherents of the 'movement', if it may yet be called such a thing, believe that the senseless drive to ever greater efficiency has taken the soul out of the pastime.

### Respect for engineering...

Although one might be forgiven for thinking that this trend is all about purchasing vintage bicycles and some do seek out functioning antiques, this is not the whole story. These bicycles are being remade in the UK by various companies such as Pashley and abroad most notably in Copenhagen by Velorbis.

The trend towards bicycles built for commuter or leisure use in the urban landscape does not stop at self-consciously kitsch remakes of the classics...

*"Fancy road and mountain bikes are clearly no longer king of the roost - or road. It's the scads of fixed-gear, town, single-speed and other urban bicycles that are drawing the crowds."*

*Eli Milchman, Wired*

It's interesting that the new(ish) 'urban' cycling category contains elegant commuter rides and sportier fixed gear / single speed bikes. The London Tweed Run saw plenty of all such bicycles being ridden with aplomb by gentlemen and ladies showing great bearing and decorum.

The Tweed Run was conceived of by the Tweed Cycling Club in conjunction with the LFGSS (London Fixed Gear & Single Speed) in London and inaugurated on a cold January morning starting at Savile Row, the spiritual home of exquisite tailoring. The ride was a leisurely ramble through London with plenty of stops for refreshment rather than an unseemly scramble to a finish line to prove some pathetic sense of superiority over one's peers.

The Tweed Run immediately sparked copycat events in several cities worldwide proving that sartorial elegance is no longer to be sniffed at in the world of the cyclist.

**Many a true word is spoken in jest...**

Is there a genuine yearning for the return of older values, which have been lost in the contemporary urban landscape, at play? Perhaps the tongue is not quite in the cheek after all.

With ever greater efforts being made by so called 'first world' governments to promote cycling as an alternative means of transport, and of course the rather discouraging expense of running a petrol powered motor vehicle, more and more people are coming back to cycling to get to work. As they enter the mysterious and tribal world of the cyclist they are quite terrified by the horrifically ugly lycra, razor sharp seats and aggressive riding position of the road cyclist. They are equally unsettled by the ungainly and expensive theatrics of the mountain bike and of course not being twelve years old they would rather not be seen in full control of their faculties riding a BMX. (Have we offended everybody yet?) Finally, although tricked out, LA style low-rider bicycles look wicked but are ridiculously uncomfortable to ride.

So where does the modern gentleman turn to find cycling solutions to fit the needs of his working life and leisure time?

Many people want to ride and yet do not wish to surrender their identity to the activity. For the gentleman or lady the city bike or single speed offer an understated style that oozes chic by virtue of its simplicity and functionality. The riders my friends are the stars of the show, the bicycle should never upstage them.

Riding all over the world

### Riding All Over the World

There's a scene that's playing out the world over from San Francisco to Barcelona, Hong Kong to Portland. Whether it's crews such as Singapore's Crank Arm Steady meeting up in Haji Lane for a snack and a tootle through the art district or Enciclika Corpus Fixie hitting Barcelona for a game of polo in 'The Asprin'. A community is coming together. The humble coffee shop and noodle bar are now the meeting place for a new breed of velo disciple. If singlespeed is the hub then the spokes radiate to every corner of the globe.

Picture the scene. It's warm and humid. A gaggle of riders are drawn to an all night store akin moths to neon, their bikes laid out like a sweetshop display by the side of the road. Anticipation is in the air. Everybody is dressed to ride. We're in Taipei and its 'Friderday'!

For those of us who don't really know where Taipei is, or even what it might be, (be honest here) let's just lay all our cards on the table before we begin. Taipei is the capital city of the Republic of China and it lies in the northern part of the island of Taiwan, an island found off the South East coast of the Chinese mainland.

As native English speaking westerners our mental furniture when it comes to China is, let's face it, a little sparse. The most I ever read about Taiwan was the 'Made in Taiwan' sticker on the back of some bargain

bin plastic toys of my youth. However, times are changing and the peoples' university (Wikipedia) is a great dispeller of ignorance.

Taipei is massive and her different neighbourhoods feature a wide variety of terrain from flat grid plan to mountainous hills with breathtaking views. Add to all that a warm climate with mild winters and a large population of young people looking for kicks and you have all the ingredients for a thriving bicycle scene.

The scenesters don't have to look far to get hold of a good ride either. Friderday is a regular Alleycat race and trick Battle organised by Nabiis. Their slogan...

"We're not in it for fashion. We're in it for the rush."

All in all, Friderday comes off as the focal point of a young, friendly and fun crowd who are definitely cool but not too cool for school.

Whether it's bombing the streets of San Francisco, trick riding in Florida or tearing the arse out of Tokyo, a single (speed) passion prevails - it's the coming together of likeminded individuals with an affection for two wheels good.

The cooling of polo

### The Cooling of Polo

Imagine if you will that you work for the kind of marketing company that is oft tasked with guerrilla marketing, viral campaigning, cool-hunting, green washing and re-branding. A mysterious client saunters in wearing jodhpurs and sporting a well waxed mustache and drops an assignment on your warm lap. The assignment? Make Polo cool.

You would have course have spat out a mouthful of your Frappuccino in horror and flatly refused. Surely nothing quite so unabashedly over privileged could ever be cool? (Sports cars and cocaine notwithstanding.)

Yet somehow the sport of kings has been stolen, Robin Hood like from the gardens of the aristocracy by that great liberator of the common man: the velocipede.

It was the hard faced Irish madman Dick McCready who first struck upon the idea of substituting the horse with a bicycle in 1891. Later on, much as in the plot of a Mel Gibson movie, the bastard English redcoats stole the idea and the first international games were played at Crystal Palace. Soon enough the cyclist nation par excellence (France) caught whiff of the new trend and came on board with aplomb. The early version of the game peaked in popularity in 1908 with a tournament held at the Olympic games no less.

The game was then sadly eclipsed by the new and unfathomably popular and obscene sport of living for months in a freezing cold muddy trench before running towards a machine gun waving a pointy stick.

After World War one (Sort of like the Olympics of killing) cycle polo came back with a vengeance, then World War 2 came back with a vengeance and the game fell into decline.

Anyway, we're not really interested in that story here. The game doesn't start to get even remotely cool until the 'hard-court' or 'urban bike polo' variant comes into existence in the late noughties. Played with smaller teams on hard courts (the original was played on grass) like municipal tennis courts, bits of road or whatever can be found, the game has been re-invented by the common street rat. The street version is fast. With no 'chukkas' (quarters) the clock just keeps running till the first team reaches five goals, or the games are given short set time limits to keep tournaments moving along.

The beauty of the game is that it's very accessible. Everything is very fresh and the chance is there for anyone to get involved and contribute. At the time of writing the nascent Barcelona scene is literally growing out of nothing. The first urban bike polo world championships kicked off in the USA so there is an exciting vibe going on. People involved really feel like they are making

something happen and making their own little mark on history. And of course, messengers play it so it's definitely cool.

Cristian "Spaceboy" Marín of Enciclika, an avid player and promoter of the game, emphasises that the European style of hardcourt polo is diverging from the US style. He explained that the across the pond, the game was similar in spirit to street hockey. It's rough and aggressive with all three players active in attack. The European game tends to use one player as a permanent defender and the style of play is more tactical. (Even so, pile ups can happen.) This could prove an impediment to the internationalisation of the game as the European teams would be at a stark disadvantage playing in the USA organised 'world' championship.

Jordi Tamayo, also of Enciclika expects that the sport will in fact evolve into distinct strands over time.

Through the efforts of the Fixa Club group Spaceboy and Tamayo have built a thriving polo scene in BCN capable of fielding several teams in the European championships and taking home fourth prize (well there was no 'prize' as such, but a glimmer of glory nonetheless). All this in a city that has no native courier culture.

Fixa Club found a bizarre arena to play in, that one can only guess was built for minor gladiatorial combat, located in the Eixample Dret side of the city. The perfectly circular dug out ring is surrounded by benches and lit up by streetlights allowing for play to go on late into the night. The club have re-christened it 'The Aspirin' presumably due to its shape. From eleven in the evening till the small hours of the morning players keep swinging those sticks. Every Monday, Wednesday and Friday night, teams can be found honing their skills in the ring; they also come to hang out, talk bikes and have a few beers on the side. On Sundays the teams test their skills on randomly selected courts around the city in order to improve their away game on foreign surfaces. It's all very social and international; players reflecting the city's cosmopolitan make-up. Teams from abroad come to see how they do it in BCN, including Pink's manager and her friends all the way from Australia.

Another interesting element of the game for the techies is that different teams use different types of bicycle. There is no rule that Polo bicycles have to be fixed wheel and the Championships in Paris saw all manner of rigs in play from

mountain bikes to road racers to track bikes to BMX. The only law is that the bike must be safe, so no stunt pegs basically. Could we end up seeing formations?

Mountain bike in defence – BMX midfield – Fixed Track Bike in attack. The 'MBF' Formation?

In London the London Single Speed / Fixed Gear club provide information for anyone wishing to get into the sport. Hardcourt Polo may never get to the Olympics in the form in which it currently exists (no referee and a loose attitude to the term 'foul') yet it looks set to blossom into an international phenomenon nonetheless. There is no better time to get involved!

## Give a man a fish . . .

Henry Thoreau said that one of the things every man should do in life is to build his own house. By 'house' Henry meant shack but we take his point. If you build a man a custom rig he'll ride a few seasons, if you teach him to build his own he'll ride for ever. Indeed, taking control of the means of production has long been held to be a powerful act and is increasingly becoming more relevant now that the global economy has been revealed for the casino run by monkeys that it is. The more skills that Joe public can rescue from the wreckage of industrial production, the better for all of us in the long run. Of course we can't really make every component in the garage but we can still glean a great deal of pleasure and pride from tailoring our own rig. The joy of riding a bike you have made from scratch is quite indescribable. One feels an almost unquenchable desire to shout out 'I made this!' as one tours about town, stopping occasionally for a latte. Go on and do it! Now the internet is there to guide you and to supply you with parts you have no more excuses. There's always time if you make time . . .

Death and the Cyclist

## Flirting with La Muerte

Much is made of the state of heightened awareness attained by the practice of riding fixed. No doubt, riding in heavy traffic with an inordinately extended stopping distance does sharpen the mind but then so, we might presume, does having a gun to one's head.

The cyclist will happily talk about the mechanics of riding fixed, the logic of it, the fun aspects but few will be so forthcoming about the simple fact that it's just plain dangerous. And danger is such a deceitful word, such a sweet and seductive word, a word that neatly avoids mentioning horrible injury or death.

*You see quite a number of people riding fixed-wheel bicycles in London, and they all have certain things in common: they are young, fit, and obviously have no preoccupation with mortality whatsoever. They believe they are going to pedal forever.*

*Will Self, 'The Independent'*

Perhaps for the majority fixed wheel cycling is a relatively\* safe 'fix' but there is a significant element within the Fixie scene that is in it for the thrill of fear.

\*In relation to say, riding a superbike or going over Niagara Falls in a barrel.

This could be deemed a 'fear kick. A deliberate pursuit in search of 'The Edge.'

*The Edge... there is no honest way to explain it because the only people who really know where it is, are the ones who have gone over.*

*Hunter S Thompson*

*...some of us have taken it straight over the high side from time to time - and there is always Pain in that... But there is also Fun, the deadly element, and Fun is what you get when you screw this monster on. BOOM! Instant take-off, no screeching or squawking around like a fool, with your teeth clamping down on your tongue and your mind completely empty of everything but fear.*

*Hunter S Thompson, Song of the Sausage Creature*

The edge is then a terrifying 'satori' or enlightenment experience in the sense of Zen as most new-age westerners wouldn't recognise it.

Then again, all cheap talk of Zen aside, we could frame this trip in another light. It could just be about fun right? Of course it could, and as we all know danger can be fun. In fact even getting hurt has a peculiar buzz to it. As someone once said (Paraphrased from the excellent movie – 'Waking Life') when the crash happened the overwhelming feeling was this – finally! Something is actually happening to me.

So why do we enjoy danger? No doubt science can offer an explanation or two...

*"To produce the fight-or-flight response, the hypothalamus activates two systems: the sympathetic nervous system and the adrenal-cortical system...The combined effects of these two systems are the fight-or-flight response.*

*...the hypothalamus releases... (CRF) into the pituitary gland, activating the adrenal-cortical system. The pituitary gland...secretes the hormone ACTH. ACTH moves through the bloodstream and ultimately arrives at the adrenal cortex, where it activates the release of approximately 30 different hormones that get the body prepared to deal with a threat."*

*How Stuff Works*

So is it all just a complicated way of getting high in the narcotic sense? Do people push the envelope simply in order to score a dose of the good shit off the greatest drug dealer of them all: the adrenal cortex?

Or is there a more political explanation for this flirtation with danger? In the annals of counter-cultural modern history it is written that 'Boredom is Political' and as every year passes our cities come to resemble Aldous Huxley's Brave New World to ever greater degrees. Small wonder that new breeds of angry young men appear, always eager to flip the bird at any square in a car who takes liberties.

*We don't want a world where the guarantee of not dying of starvation brings the risk of dying of boredom.*

*Paris '68 Graffito*

So what if, for the sake for argument we frame this culture as a deliberate act of resistance against the tyranny of the motor vehicle. Is there anything in that?

It might seem strange to identify leftist politics with anti-car sentiment given the ubiquitous nature of 'people's cars' in communist Europe. However, as early as the 1950's the Surrealists were denouncing the motor vehicle as a prison cell on wheels, a mere extension of the state of slavery designed to make labour more efficient.

London's 'Reclaim the Streets' set out to rid the streets of old England of motor vehicles back in the early 1990's and although their agenda was politically broad (the transformation of everyday life no less) their focus was the tyranny of the motor vehicle. The group pioneered methods of peaceably forcing roads to close and staging protests that were effectively celebrations rather than angry rants. From this milieu the British critical mass cycling movement sprung. (It is believed that the first critical mass rides took place in San Francisco)

Critical mass bike rides are now used as a form of protest/celebration in 300 cities all over the world. Critical mass rides are however, a very conscious expression of political dissent. The riders involved have thrown their hats in the political ring, have they have declared the car and everything it signifies as an enemy? (to varying degrees of course). What of the lone cyclist or rookie courier without political agenda? What of the man or woman who starts riding to work for the first time? A perhaps previously happy relationship with the motor vehicle is then brought into sharp relief. Consider the following snapshot, if you will...

Suddenly the beady eye of the cyclist, fizzing like a bare wire on a cocktail of thirty different hormones, fixes upon the puffy visage of the motorist, who in turn is barely awake and in this moment we see a reflection of the terse and uneasy relationship between the mammal and the dinosaur. There is a natural line of enmity here, which for all efforts to the contrary is still mortally disputed.

It's a dispute that cyclists are at present losing. (At this point let it be made abundantly clear that from here on we are talking about cyclists in general and not specifically 'thrill-seekers'.)

**Cars don't kill people - people do.**

Even as governments promote cycling as a balm to the environmental ravages of the petrol dependant society, cyclists are still suffering on the roads of the world's major cities.

Ultimately the problem is the mentality of road users and in particular, the attitude of motorists. Inside a fully enclosed vehicle the driver feels as if he is in an extension of his own house. Everywhere is then his territory and everybody around him is therefore a nuisance. Seeing life through windscreen panes, framed by the chassis puts the driver into the mental state of a passive observer. It's like watching TV. Motorists are not really aware of the forces at play, they don't feel their velocity, they are not fully present while they fiddle with the radio dial and surreptitiously answer their phones.

If all that sounds unfair then consider the figures...

In the UK most efforts to reduce road accidents via public awareness campaigns are frequently directed at drunk drivers. Yet back in 2007 driving under the influence represented only 6% of all road casualties.

The more considerable figure is perhaps the 35% of accidents caused by, wait for it . . .the driver not looking. (Can you imagine a cyclist not looking?)

You can bet that this comes as no surprise to the average bicycle messenger. The menace of dooring (having a door opened in ones path while cycling at high speeds) is well documented. What is less well known is that it is actually illegal in most countries to open a door without looking. However, prosecution in cases that involve either cyclist injury or even death is incredibly rare. The attitude is such that the events are almost universally reported as 'accidents' and in some cases it is even implied that the cyclist should really have been wearing a helmet anyway so it's kind of their fault.

Of the many dangers that face the cyclist the truck is perhaps the worst. Buffalo Bill of Moving Target runs a campaign specifically to improve the situation that has claimed around seven lives in London back in 2007 (figures are difficult to verify). The campaign did win some significant concessions and legal reform.

*"Now, 4 years after Seb's death, all new lorries, starting this summer, will have to be fitted with a 4th mirror that eliminates the blind-spot left and front... This mirror will also eliminate the most common excuse of defence lawyers in court – that the cyclist was in the driver's blind-spot.*

*There is also a new offence of causing death by careless driving, which carries much more appropriate penalties (in my view) for the crime of negligently killing another road-user."*

*Buffalo Bill, Moving Target*

Proof then if it were needed that political pressure can produce concrete results and encouragement for those who currently campaign for better conditions for cyclists.

Similar campaigns exist all over the world and the one which has captured the imagination of the press with its quietly powerful visual statements is the Ghost Bike Memorial Project.

*Ghost Bikes are dignified and sombre memorials for bicyclists killed on the streets of New York City. A bicycle painted all white is locked near the crash site accompanied by a small plaque remembering the fallen cyclist.*

*The New York City Street Memorial Project*

BICYCLING
A JOYFUL STATEMENT
FOR PEACE

COMMITTEE FOR FULL ENJOYMENT

*The sound of a car door opening in front of you*
*is similar to the sound of a gun being cocked . . .*
*Amy Webster*

The first Ghost Bikes were placed in Missouri in 2003 and since then the practice has spread to more than 75 cities worldwide. The New York group reveals some shocking figures not just for cyclists but also pedestrians. 166 pedestrians were killed by motor vehicles in New York city in one year (2006). At the time of writing there are 59 ghost bikes in place in NYC.

*We're not yelling for bike lanes. What we're looking for is a little more intangible. We're hoping that the culture changes...*

*Rachael Myers, former NYC Street Memorial Project Volunteer*

So do we believe that the culture can change? Let's hope so. Motorists need to recognise the rights of cyclists to use the road. It's not a question of segregated spaces; it's a question of mutual respect. Well perhaps not quite mutual. Cyclists will always be fitter and more sexually attractive than motorists. At least they have that.

But isn't it ironic that the beautiful ones who ride fixed for thrills have simply embraced the risks? Perhaps it's because they know the dark truth about riding safely . . .

Never trust a motor vehicle.

## The Pistapocalypse
## - Visions of a Self Propelled Future

What is the Pistapocalypse? The simple answer is that we just don't know. Scholars maintain that the real meaning was lost centuries ago. Others still claim that it is a catastrophe of transportation foretold by the Mayan calendar. Well if the Mayans were so damn clever where is their big willy civilisation now eh? All of this aside, we can no longer afford to be flippant about this extinction level event.

In recent years we've come to realise that just like every great empire ours too will soon crumble into a pathetic shadow of its former world spanning glory. We have failed, and all that now remains is self-denial, debauchery and suffering. So we must ask ourselves - what next for bicycles?

When society collapses we'll need to make sure that we know how to get the maximum longevity out the bicycle parts that we already have. However, mid to long term we will need to stock pile information on how to actually build components too. If cycling is to survive the collapse of capitalism, peak oil and carbon capping then we need to be able to build bicycles from scratch without damaging the environment in the process or spending any money.

We will also need to start thinking of the bicycle as a primary mode of transportation. We'll need ambulances, fire trucks, school buses and such to be replaced by groups of hardy youngsters riding cycle based contraptions of epic ingenuity. We'll build a brave new world wheel by wheel where everyone who can ride will, and indeed all electricity will be generated this way too.

So get thinking people. It's only a matter of time before the oil runs out . . .

### Does art and creative interpretation tie into riding a single speed or fixed gear?

I guess it depends on how you sell it really. I could make it into this big awe inspiring world effecting doing you part type thing speech, which I'm sure a lot of the companies would like to hear or it could just be about just getting out there and fuckin' riding! It's not about SS or FG. It's about your love for what you're doing in this moment right now. It's about being out there sweating your balls off, private bits torn asunder, wondering when it's going to be your turn to have friends visiting you in the hospital because it seems like 90% of the motor vehiclists are doing everything it is in their power to kill or maim you. To me it's more about the thrill of making it through another day unscathed..

The only real art I see in it is in your own creative way of interpreting the pain and suffering you put yourself

## You Think You Look Normal?

It's been said that it is a crazy man's game, a fool's parade, and an unwise enterprise to ride Fixed gear. And yet what are the alternatives? Do you think you look normal out there on your road racer? Hm?

For generations cycling has meant, for most people, engaging in the bizarre and ritualistic act of self flagellation that is road racing. Those men (and they are mostly men) who stuff their whole bodies into luminous condoms to spend hours on end sucking exhaust fumes straight out of the tail pipes of passing lorries are lauded as heroes while the eminently more sensible Fixie rider is accused of lunacy purely for riding a track bike around town. It makes no sense. Consider again the nature of their sport.

The standard for even the semi-pro in road racing is so dizzyingly high that even though these amateur fans will gladly subject themselves to gruelling ninety kilometre treks before breakfast they will still never be contenders.

It doesn't look cool. Only a die-hard fan would claim that it looks cool and then from a skewed viewpoint indeed. It looks painful.

And finally, it's not even significantly safer than riding Fixies is it? OK so the Fixed Gear aficionado is jumping a few red lights in town but out there on the dual cariageway your time trialling roadie is pedalling away with a stream of lorries passing him less than a meter away at speeds of 70 mph. Who is safer?

(Disclaimer: This article has its tongue 'in its cheek' we love those crazy condom guys really!).

Alleycat songs for underground cats

## Alleycat songs for Underground Cats

Big Sport belongs to 'The Man'. These days every game that once graced the street corner is now professionalised, commercialised, repackaged and syndicated via pay per view. Ordinary folk have no place in sport. Tour de France supermen train literally every day; while weak and feeble mortals take time off to spend with their families citing pathetic excuses like, 'It's Christmas Day'. Do you think Lance spends Christmas day stuffing his face with poultry and fine wines? No way Jose. He's out on the bike.

Small wonder then that the prowling figure of the Alleycat has struck such a chord with those who still have the energy and will to engage in competitive activities of a physical nature and yet cannot reconcile their self-image with the quasi-religious ascetic stance of the professional athlete.

The Alleycat: lithe, wild, driven by instinct, steered by cunning; a creature of wiry musculature, sexual stench and violent displays of territoriality; a creature whose lunatic songs strike fear into children's hearts and call the wild ones out to play...

It's easy to picture how these races first came staggering into their twilight existence. The bicycle messenger culture was beginning to consolidate around a few organisations and a bar or two (Toronto, c1989.) As boozed up messengers began more and more to hang out in the same seedy drinking holes as one another (remember that these creatures are tomcats whether ostensibly female or not) cat fights exploded over spilt jars of snakebite black. Who was the fastest!? Who was the most cunning? Who knew this district or that better than anyone? And moreover, who had the biggest balls and the meanest heart!?

The matter had to be settled on the streets, and so the first events were organised. Soon enough, through the medium of the CMWC (A kind of black Sabbath ritual) the Canuk vets of the savage early races bragged the phenomena into international existence.

The races mirror the skill set required of a pro-courier with a few diabolical twists thrown in for good measure. Racers are given a list of check points before the race much the same way a courier

receives a daily manifest. The checkpoints often include themed tasks ranging from the sublime to the powerfully alcoholic.

Few seem to care about winning and generally it's the locals who do win as knowledge of the area is an enormous advantage. It's not difficult for event organisers to blag prizes from cool brands and sometimes it can even be worth the effort to win. Regardless of who does win sooner or later the thing turns into a drinking session. Often sooner.

The semi-legal status of the event, the messenger history and above all: the spoke cards all serve to make the Alleycat the coolest of sports currently available to urban humanity. Should The Man ever get hold of it, he'll have a hard time televising an event where the racers warm up with a smoke and a tin of McDuffs Special Ale. The moral majority would crawl off their armchairs in uproar and drag their enormous bulks to the telephone to send in a torrent of complaints to the broadcaster without shadow of a doubt. Meanwhile those young gods in professional cycling who supposedly provide aspirational models for the World of Warcraft generation, just keep on jacking up that Belgian mix . . .

# 10 reasons the Cult of Fixed rubs some cats up the wrong way

We're assuming you're an acolyte of The Cult of Fixed, (which is a safe bet) unless

a) you're reading this book while seated on the porcelain throne at a friend's house and said friend is a bit partial to the Fixed disposition, or

b) your mother mistakenly bought you this book not realising that you're actually a mountain biker.

Putting those possibilities aside it can't have escaped your notice that some people are a little bit...how can we put this? Some people are a teency bit aggrieved by fixed gear track bike culture.

So in the interests of scientific research we at 42x12 set out to investigate what it is that the innocent Fixie Fanatic has done to deserve all this perjury. We bravely sent our best (work experience boy) researchers out to wade through the seething bitchiness of the online cycling community and found the following ten answers. The results are presented in ascending order from the mildly offensive to the most pista-profane level of velo-blashpemy.

Take this as you will but be warned, it is not for the faint of heart...

## 10 The Top Tube Bar

The top tube, gently cosseted in the soft embrace of a foam pad lovingly invites one to take greater risks because should the unthinkable happen, and a high speed convergence of testicles and top tube become a sudden, chilling reality – the pad will somehow make it all alright.

Aside from the fact that one shouldn't be performing tricks on a track bike at all – because it's made of coat hangers and it's designed for riding on a polished track – and because it's simply undignified – these bits of foam are clearly fashion accessories and are thus despicable to any real cyclist.

## 09 The Mag Wheel

Installing one 'Mag Wheel' is very much the cycling equivalent of buying two pairs of trainers and wearing a different one on each foot. It does happen, it is technically cool according to all the official criteria and it may even look pretty slick but ultimately it is kryptonite to the genuine velo-head. If you are going to waste time and money finding and installing said wheel purely for aesthetic reasons you have already demonstrated to the world that you are a shallow and weak person concerned only with surface appearances. You are incorrect. You must leave, now.

## 08 Spoke Cards

Once again it is the sin of in-authenticity that haunts the seemingly innocent and naive act of sticking cards in your spokes. Affixing ornaments to your spokes, like an excited child rushing outside with a free gift from the cereal box to attach to your wheels, plays to the onlooker as a sickeningly knowing and contrived act, because you are an adult.

And that is just how it reads to the uniformed passer-by. Those few heads who actually know or care what spoke cards represent hate you even more. Why? Because you have never been in an alleycat race; you bought them off eBay.

## 07 Track Stands

It almost seems unfair to disparage the humble track stand and yet, as the most visible symbol of the cult it is one of the most despised. On a basic level the track stand is simply the most practical way to remain stationery on a Fixie for a brief period of time while waiting for the lights to change. Given that many Fixed Wheel heads consider themselves above traffic laws such as red light stops shouldn't the track stand be applauded?

No. The track stand is evil. It is simply a way for the rider to (metaphorically) bellow to the world through a megaphone: I am Ozymandias and I RIDE FIXED, LOOK UPON ME YE MIGHTY AND DESPAIR.

The track stand has also become seen as a trick in its own right, which takes us from the sublime to the ridiculous. What is the audience supposed to get from the awesome feat of remaining still for a bit? I'd rather watch a fat kid do a 'Rubik's Cube' really fast.

### 06 Handlebars

Leave the handlebars alone. The only quantifiable result of shearing off the better part of your handle bars, is an uglier bike. This is only compounded by wrapping them up in ten rolls of tape. Doing both then describing them as 'upgrades' on craigslist and subsequently listing your bike for a higher price tag than it originally cost because you spent your precious time shearing off the handlebars, is an act so far off the scale of Fixed Lunacy that we're not even mad, we're impressed. Carry on.

### 05 Funemployed

They don't hate you because you're a hipster, secretly they hate you because you are over privileged and therefore have no concept of work, suffering or value. That's what they mean when they say 'hipster', they mean 'rich kid'. You have everything, but that does not satisfy you because you don't even notice it, instead you crave the one thing you don't have and that's authenticity. This is why you try to adopt a rebel pose and seek risks in order to prove yourself. This is why you get obsessed with whatever sub-culture you can find. Aggressively riding your track bike all day does not prove how real you are, it simply proves that you don't need to work for a living and that makes the rest of us jealous. There it is.

### 04 They Can't Ride for Shizzle

Fixed is attracting many new adherents to the creed of cycling. This is a blessing and a curse.

People who are not used to riding even a nice simple city bike are suddenly riding precarious, confusing, counter intuitive and dangerous bicycles all over the town. They don't know the rules of the road and they lack even basic skills such as looking over the shoulder or taking one hand off the bars to signal. This makes the road more dangerous for everybody and helps to aggravate the ever present resentment motorists already feel for cyclists.

### 03 Brand Fetishism

Hipsters are the worst and most unholy of all capitalists. They seek out authenticity wherever it hides and corrupt it into the stinking, foul fetish of brand worship with its triplet gospels of unbridled materialism, snobbery and greed. Any human activity is reduced to shopping and all culture becomes commercial activity under the baleful gaze of the hungry ghosts of western post industrial capitalist life. Comrades we must...! Oops, wrong meeting. Ahem.

### 02 Fakenger

'Fakenger' is very nearly the worst depth to which the Fixie Fad sinks; this is the wholesale theft of all the cultural symbols of the bicycle messenger community. Hard working, hard drinking package slinging road warriors the world over have built, with only their blood sweat and gears, a global culture worthy of great respect. And now the whole thing has been gate-crashed by mac-book-toting, spindly-legged tossers who spend more time in Starbucks than they ever do at work. Get a job and get your own style.

### 01 They don't f*©%ing RIDE them

There can be no greater sin. Nobody wants to see five hundred dollar bicycles being wheeled around the city on foot. Nobody wants to see it. Donate the thing to someone who might actually use it!

My main focus with cycling, collecting and artistic endeavours geared towards cycling, is to entertain and ensnare the viewer. To convey an emotional response, to infuse a feeling amongst the cycling community that invokes inspiration and initiative along with the overwhelming desire to do more, do better, give back, ride more, build and destroy something, then build it again! Abduct someone from their monotonous day in day out lives and remind them just how good it feels to be on the road with playful banter and a coasting freewheel as the soundtrack . . .

*Alan Sikiric, NYC*

Intricate lugs are like a really great set of tits. Not easily obtained but greatly appreciated when in the hands of a true connoisseur . . .

*Alan Sikiric, NYC*

**Facetious tips from the old school pro peloton**

Interested in raising your game with the application of dangerous, illegal drugs? To make your own 'Belgian Mix' simply blend cocaine, heroin, caffeine, amphetamines and whatever analgesics you can get your hands on. It's best to mainline the mix straight into a major vein with a hypodermic. If you haven't got any needles then just have a look around the nearest patch of urban wasteland and you'll probably find a few lying around. That'll give you a fighting chance in the next alleycat race. Although you'll probably be awake for about four days after that. Actually it's probably best to stick with two cans of Bud and a ten pack of Malboro.

## The Death of Fixie

Declaring something to be dead is generally a good sign that it's getting popular. It's always worked for musicians, artists and poets so why not for bicycles? The sooner we can declare fixed gear legally dead the better. So what are the criteria for the clinical death of a cycling subculture and how can we recognise them? There is, as ever, some dispute about this.

Richard Caseby of 'The Times' had a good stab at it citing the interest of middle aged columnists Will Self and AA Gill as proof that the scene was dying. All well and good if you're British but that ain't going to fly in the States unless Gill and Self are as transatlantically famous as the White Album. And even then nobody in Taipei is going to give a flying monkey about what type of bicycle an admittedly fine English science fiction writer is currently riding. Maybe if Boris Johnson (go google) could be persuaded to ride a Fixie then Caseby would be onto a winner . . .

More hopefully it was recently noted that someone had posted on a notorious fixed gear forum asking for advice for how to change a fixed gear rig back into a single speed. It's yet to be seen if this was the high water mark or just a statistical blip.

Another blogger, this time based in Washington DC explains that the life cycle of a scene can be seen to be in decline when it appears in the Washington Post. By the time the Post gets around to recognising that something is cool it simply isn't cool anymore. And the Post put a 1700 word nail into the Fixie coffin back in September 2009.

Is this enough? Almost, but the one thing that remains to really kill the thing is probably what you have in your hands right now. The coffee table book! By now there are probably half a dozen such titles on Amazon so we can safely say that the game is over. You can get back to enjoying you're Fixie without having to worry about being trendy anymore. And we can all feel proud to have helped out in this kind little act of cultural euthanasia.

Congratz playa!!!

Where fashion follows function

### Where Fashion follows Function

A gap has opened in the almighty 'market' as more and more people come to cycling carrying with them an elevated fashion sensibility on a hipper tip. Now those same hips don't want to be seen stripped bare as their standard denim slips down past 'the tip of the crevice of human shame' (by which I do mean 'ass crack') at an inopportune moment due to the aggressive riding position of one's new track bike. So, just as the gap between the cheeks is revealed so then is the gap in the cycling fashion market. Rushing in to fill said gap (the latter that is) a small yet bijous flock of designer labels have sallied forth with some highly functional high fashion with scant regard for the major sports brands and their bandwagon jumping hip-by-association hijacking of the fixie.

At the higher end of the new 'spoke couture' scene comes the denim fetish cult known as Self Edge working in collaboration with the equally quasi-religious Iron Heart to produce a purpose built cycling jean. Like most of the new jeans being released in this field this model sports a skinny legged cut below the knee. This means that all those chaps wearing luminous yellow bicycle clips can now happily toss them aside at last, as they need never fear tangling up their threads in their chain set again. Hurrah! Further advantages include the high waistline at the rear to protect the general public from the provocative and arousing vision

of a passing cyclist's sweaty arse, and of course a special pocket for the ubiquitous U-Lock.

As one might expect, particularly in the United States where men fear fashion, do not dance and resolve arguments with pistols rather than wit, the reception to 'spoke couture' has been in some circles (circles where people ride bicycles) about as warm as Scotland. Bicycle messengers simply can't afford to spend 360 USD on a pair of jeans. And if they aren't wearing them then they can't possibly be cool.

On the other hand, some people who like cycling have proper jobs and not all the new cycling jeans are at such a high price point. Why not take advantage of a purpose built cycling jean if you can? Self Edge admits that they target the denim fetishist and they sell the heaviest denim known to humanity designed for a lifetimes wear. The small LA based company SWRVE offer functional cycling jeans with similar features for a much more affordable price. More options are cropping up all the time.

Leaving behind us for a moment all the exotic promise of the cycling jean lets cast a little light on the rest of the wheel man's attire, for surely he doth not wear the pants alone?

Of course not, but it seems that the man on the fixed wheel bike knows exactly what to stick his foot inside already, and that is the footwear of a company named mysteriously after a common workman´s vehicle – Vans. They're just the right shape, they´re not too pricey and they've always been cool. Vans do of course know exactly how cool they are and they do a hell of a lot of research to make sure that the stay that way so of course they respond to cyclists adopting their footwear with custom ranges specifically for looking slick at that bike polo tournament that was probably also sponsored by Vans in the first place.

However, not all Fixie heads are ex-skateboarders who still listen to AC/DC and thankfully the gentleman cyclist has at last been catered for. Oozing gentlemanly deportment and probably smelling of Pimms on a summer afternoon in Maidenhead, Quoc Pham leather, tailored bicycling foot-holders (shoes) have arrived. These delectable cow skin constructions look too good to even wear and should probably just be kept in a display case above the hearth of your front room, a room no doubt clad in rich mahogany.

Moving swiftly on, as if transported by a pair of dashing Quoc Pham magic slippers, we come to the unavoidable topic of the messenger bag. No other cycling orientated garment has caused such heartache, cross and ribald interchanges of harsh words and other such conflict in the manner known to the south east English as 'Handbags at Dawn'. What is the bone of contention? People who are not messengers use messenger bags. Worse still, some people who don't even ride bikes use them!

Well so what? They're cool and hordes of producers compete to produce ever cooler models at increasingly expensive price points. These days it takes teams of cultural scientists using highly sophisticated cool detection software to keep up with which messenger bag brand one should be wearing at the precise moment; perhaps a trifle decadent for an accessory that by its very nature should be built to endure years of service.

Caps on the other hand are like candy and even messengers can afford them. It's one of the few garments that fixie heads wear that is reminiscent of the stylistic concerns of the more traditional cycling geek. By which I mean that it looks like the old French cycling caps from back in the day that those Tour de France types get off on. Ranging from expensive to cheap as chips and in a huge array of styles the cap is a great entry point for those who want to say to the world "Hey I ride bikes and I'm cool as fuck." And the coolest of the cool would have to be the Keirin style...

Finally, if you really want to take Functional Fashion to its logical extreme (while perhaps quietly dropping the Fashionable part by the roadside on the way) then it's time for you to meet the Bike Suit. Bike Suit is the Terminator Exo-Skeleton of Cycling Fashion. The suit is designed for the urban velowarrior who absolutely will not get the bus to work unless he is dead. The suit won a Eurobike Award in 2009 simply for scaring the living shit out of the judges. The prototype unfortunately had to be withdrawn after it took control of the wearer and gave him inhuman strength, destroying several petrol driven vehicles in the parking lot before being taken down by police snipers. The suit is now finally available to the general public.

Enjoy.

The anatomy of a hater

### The anatomy of a hater

"Like, where are all the negative vibes coming from dude?"

The internet is awash with fierce hyperbole directed squarely at any innocent young hipster who might dare to ride fixed gear without acquiring some sort of licence first.

Yes, granted much of this prose is quite funny (See SF Weekly – 'Ask a Track Bike') but then again a lot of it is not (See Manolith – '13 Reasons Why the Fixies Fad Should End Now!').

It often sounds just a little bit too much like the writer is truly seething with rage to be believable as a piece of hilarious satire. One wonders if these guys can sleep at night for the venom eating out their insides that has been so innocently engendered by the rise of the 'Fixie' stereotype.

Without wishing to pander to the ridiculous notion that some people might be getting into cycling for 'the wrong reasons' we can perhaps allow that some people are more interested in acquiring cool status than actually cycling. However, more than enough digital ink has been spilled in detailing the anatomy of such criminals, who incidentally will remain oblivious to any criticism anyway. Instead, let's focus for a moment on the anatomy of the Fixie Hater...

*"It seems to be a sad fact that every "underground" fashion scene will inevitably be taken over by pretentious wannabes."*

...yes indeed, thus the writer neatly putting themselves forward as poster boy for hater species number one, the 'JPS' or 'Just Plain Spiteful'. Let's analyse the crux of the argument. The big clue here is the use of the term wannabe. (BTW that means – 'Want to be') So the problem with the underground fashion scene is that people who want to be underground and fashionable will be attracted to it...

There is the paradox of 'cool' in a nutshell. If you want to be cool, you aren't. This explains the motivation for loudly proclaiming how lame it is to be cool. It is supposed to demonstrate how cool you are.

The writer is clearly a sociological genius. They are also, clearly not a cyclist so why they so passionately defend supposedly AUTHENTIC cultural symbols such as messengers is not clear. Hang on a minute, it is clear – they're just plain spiteful and furthermore have learned that people will afford them attention if they express their spite in an exaggerated way.

The response to such blog posts from actual fixie riders commonly follows a similar line of argument to that presented by 'Phil' in a comment on the aforementioned blog.

*". . . I ride a fixed. It's fun. I ride it a lot . . ."*

A debate winner if ever there was one.

Hater number two is a cut above your JPS and an altogether more complicated creature. These people are the real cycle heads who see the Fixie newbie as an unwelcome entrant into the hallowed world of the bicycle. These are the 'Real Heads'.

*"...do not make the mistake that hipsters are making a choice in riding track bikes — they are merely stealing other people's choices. And Carter, remember what God said: Thou shalt not steal."*

These are guys who have been involved in cycling for a long time. Or at least they have been involved in cycling for a long time relative to how long they've been alive. A chap at the age of twenty still thinks two years is a long time.

These guys are horrified that the hip factor of the fixed gear scene is attracting (Shock! Horror!) newbies.

It is a well worn observation that the revolution often becomes the establishment. One can even hear old ravers complain that the grindcore of today ain't like the good honest happy hardcore of yesteryear. The fact that ecstasy addled merry pranksters who have spent the last fifteen years with their head in a bass bin now feel that they have earned the right to complain about newbies reveals that this is perhaps a universal trend in human nature.

When people complain about newbies all they are essentially saying is . . .

"Hey but this is our thing you know. This is like who I am."

Of course when you put effort into being different and then somebody copies you it rather undermines your intended statement. But never mind! Surely this is what drives cultural innovation?

No?

Well anyway, school them young ones if you feel the need.

It's your scene ain't it?

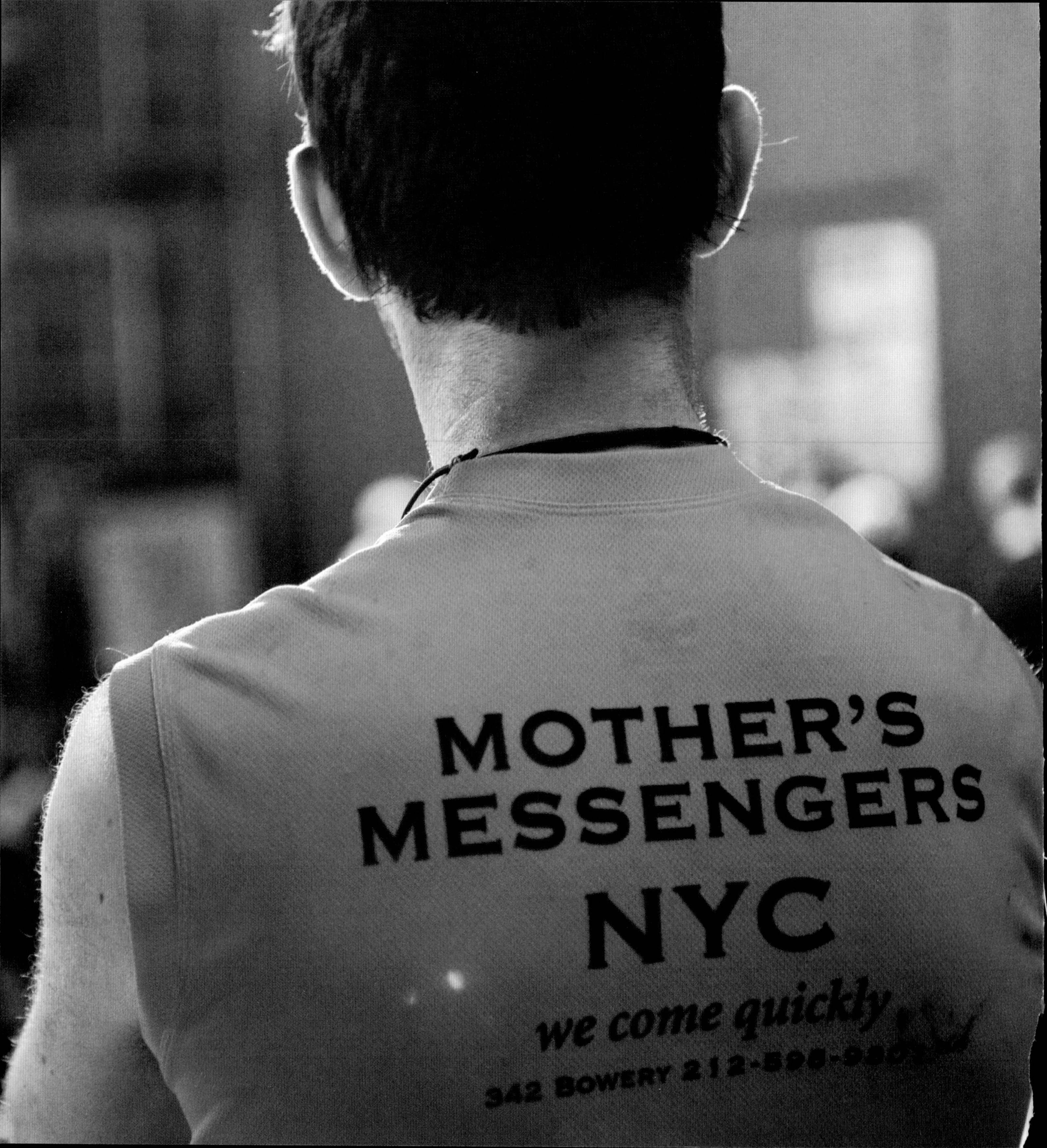
MOTHER'S
MESSENGERS
NYC
we come quickly
342 BOWERY

The courier

## The Courier

The wiry and wild-eyed figure shot through the narrow gap, briefly visible twixt the thunderous blur of traffic, propelled only by its angular thighs interacting furiously with a thin zigzag of wheeled metal. Indeed, had you been close enough to observe the creature's expression you might have remarked upon the similarity that it shared with a hunted animal.

In the city the aptly named sedentary lifestyles have swallowed all glimmer of youthly vigour and the sharp musculature of these creatures stands in stark relief against petrol junkies encased in mobile living rooms, trading their souls for comfort and security.

Our hero eschews the cycle lane for reasons only a veteran cyclist would understand. Having to daily calculate how to minimize the risk of mortal injury has made him a shrewd tactician and no pretty little cycle lane can lure him easily into trusting against his own judgement. The motorists around him are almost universally half asleep and should they behave unexpectedly, and they will always behave unexpectedly, he must be ready. With no contract and no health insurance even a minor injury can cost him dearly.

This then is the legendary courier. Or at least this is the idea of the courier that so attracts the admiration of those who would seek to stick it to 'the man'. A hard riding, hard drinking strong and manically energetic counter-cultural-hero provides for many a role model, a blueprint for a functioning way of life that circumvents the preached necessity of submitting to the grinding tedium of white collar slavery. Delivering packages may be slavery too, but at least its good honest slavery for a strong character with a quick wit.

*"You can't control the day. The man controls the day. But we will, control the bikes!"*

'The Warriors', Deliberately Misquoted by Pat

The near sexual excitement that these road ninja's inspire has perhaps not surprisingly bred a horde of aspirants and acolytes who wish to worship at the feet of the young gods of urban cycling, largely by imitating their style if not their chosen form of earning a living.

Some years past, the genuine (but now ex) courier legend 'Buffalo Bill' of 'Moving Target' infamy coined the term 'Fakenger' to describe those who would follow the ways of the courier without taking it quite so far as to actually deliver packages for money. The reactions of real messengers ranged from horror to derision, from dumbstruck confusion to bitter mirth. It was as if hipsters had started dressing like asbestos removal workers or African diamond miners. A job with the same apparent social status as a bin man (with better benefits, more holidays and a permanent contract the bin man arguably has the better deal) had miraculously acquired a following.

Now everyone knows that the internet was invented for two main reasons; the first being for practising the art of one handed typing and the second being for arguing in forums. And lo the forums did see an unholy civil war erupt between the Fakengers and the real deal...

"Shut the f*** up all you courier wannabe pussies! everybody knows that you are not a real messenger unless you ride a black track bike with no brakes, push a 52-15 gear ratio or larger, earn at least 150 bucks a day, and have suffered through at least 5 winters, until then you are just a rookie…"

*as quoted on movingtargetzine.com*

The writer may well have a valid point. But perhaps we shouldn't be so quick to judge. To be fair there aren't that many jobs available. Even if there were, the culture that has grown up around the messengers is highly attractive for many reasons. The camaraderie of working a tough job together, the social aspects, the races and games, all these things are largely missing from most jobs in the white collar age. The service industry may offer very comfortable chairs to sit in and centrally heated office blocks but it does not offer any real sense of community.

Couriers may not have a pension to look forward to but at least they've got an identity that means something.

## Will the Real Courier Please Stand Up?

Kevin Bacon's stint as a heroic bike messenger in shambolic eighties flick 'rarara' aside, the alluring counter cultural symbol of the messenger is perhaps more urban legend than urban reality. (Kevin Bacon is of course an urban reality.)

Real messengers are actually real guys and girls doing a pretty thankless and tough job who may not necessarily think it is 'cool' that they nearly get squished by trucks or ripped in half by dozy punters opening car doors without looking, during their average working day.

*Most bicyclists in New York City obey instinct far more than they obey the traffic laws, which is to say that they run red lights, go the wrong way on one-way streets, violate cross-walks, and terrify innocents, because it just seems easier that way. Cycling in the city, and particularly in midtown, is anarchy without malice.*

Author unknown, from New Yorker, "Talk of the Town"

It's not a casual exaggeration to say that the job really is dangerous. The problem of sharing the road is of course not unique to messengers and a whole array of organisations campaign internationally for greater awareness of and tolerance for cyclists. Tolerance? Yes, it seems that many drivers are actively intolerant of people who dare to use their muscles instead of spending every waking moment with their fat asses glued to a seat as they shuttle from one drive through to another.

That dangerous jobs exist in this day and age seems vaguely anachronistic. Or at least in most of the G20 territories we have developed modern solutions for dangerous industrial work. We invite first generation immigrants to do it.

Couriers are then, fairly unique in being voluntarily involved in a job that carries a serious risk of injury.

That does raise the question, why are they doing it then?

*"...the educated, middle-class, white male who rides a fixed-gear bike, dresses distinctively, doesn't wear a helmet and is attracted to risk."*

*Prof. Kevin Wehr, C.S.U.S, from an interview with Sena Christian*

Surely well-brought-up white boys with full citizenship are not risking their lives on the roads to deliver parcels here in the west in the 21st century?

Who are these aliens?

It seems off key to suggest that these guys are all borderline sociopathic when they come together so resoundingly to pull off events such as the annual CMWC.

For a bunch of guys and girls who earn at the most seventy odd Euros a day, these couriers can sure rig up a jamboree. Undeterred by earthly obstacles, hundreds of messengers travel to the annual Courier World Cycling Championships from countries all over the world to wherever the event might be held. This is grass roots organisation at its most impressive and no small part of the reason the courier world continues to attract fans. It is the wild cat writ large upon an international canvas.

The 2009 version held in Odaiba, Tokyo featured men's and women's races, sprints, track stand competitions, backward cycling and a category simply titled Fixie King & Queen. The organisation was headed up by a lovely chap known as Yoshi and the event scored backing from innumerable cool brands such as Specialized, Dickies and Adidas.

Is there any other job left in the big bad west that offers that kind of social life? It all makes the office picnic look a little bit pedestrian.

In spite of all this campaigning, unionisation and international organisation it is said that the age of the bicycle messenger as a feature of the urban landscape is numbered. The real number of jobs available is shrinking and new couriers have to do a lot of hustling to get into the game. Beard stroking cultural commentators  (such as people who write coffee table books) cite the primacy of the internet as the main reason why physical packages will soon be unnecessary.

While it is true that the digitisation of most legal systems has taken a bite of the couriers' client base,  it's unlikely that the job will be entirely eclipsed. In fact, while we're in the business of making glib predictions we may as well throw our hat in the ring and say that there will always be a demand for a hand to hand delivery service. After all, you can't email objects...yet.

## Evolution or Commercialisation?

For the originals the Fixie thing was a DIY culture. It was never about buying the most expensive brand name Fixie because for one thing, back in the day you couldn't buy such a cycle. It was about knocking together your own bicycle out of parts. Increasingly that's changing and for the majority of Fixie riders now it's much easier to get someone else to make you a bike than have to learn all the skills to do it yourself.

Of course it didn't take too long for the big brand manufacturers to get in on the scene. So what's happening now is that the brands are looking to identify different streams of Fixie culture in order to build products that are tilted towards specific patterns of usage. We can imagine that soon we'll be seeing a *'Insert Brand Here'* Fixie Alley Cat Racer, a Fixie Urban Polo or a Fixie Trick Bike.

The cynical among us might be tempted to say that this diversification is an old marketing trick to create ever more reasons to shift that price bracket higher and broaden the market further. However there is another argument that suggests that the Fixie Trick Bike is a natural and inevitable development.

In John Prolly's excellent article "FIXED FREESTYLE EVOLUTION" for Urban Velo magazine, Prolly paints an altogether different picture of the move towards purpose built fixies. He suggests that the riders themselves drove the rigs towards tougher components by a process of natural selection as over the last few years riders have tested the limits of the Fixie as a possible trick bike. In the end we are left wondering if this process may yet produce the bicycle of our time just as the BMX was the bike of the eighties.

The Fixie is in fact, no longer a track bike. It's become something different. It serves as a middle ground between the bike as a useful mode of urban transportation and the bike as a toy, a playful way to interact with the city. And with that formula it seems unlikely to disappear as quickly as many predict.

## Where did all the bargains go?

Once upon a time, three years ago, you could go into a shop and dig out some dusty old frame and take it home for less cash money than a courier earns in a day. These days even the old guys with the independent shops know they can charge an arm and a leg for a classic track bike frame. The bargains have gone and the market has wised up. Enthusiasts throwing together a rig with a few dollars and a few spare parts have been replaced by buyers willing to shell out a grand or more.

So is it really game over for the affordable Fixie? Perhaps not. Here's a couple of tips sourced from an insider. Firstly, forget track bikes and start looking out for eighties road racer frames. They're more or less the same shape and haven't yet acquired the aura of cool that's driven the prices up elsewhere. Secondly, if you can find out where the pro teams train you're on to a winner. Seek out the shops along the route and you can find bargains that the teams have discarded during their training sessions.

Finally, just keep asking questions. Everybody's grandad had a track bike (in Europe at least) and those frames have got to be gathering dust in somebody's garage/attic/yard. Try and get some of those old timers down the local watering hole involved in a session of misty eyed reminiscence, buy them bag of pipe tobacco and charm your way into their affections. It's the only way forward.

Happy hunting!

## Modern life is rubbish

People talk about tomorrow. There is no such thing. It's always now, always has been, always will be. When you're a kid it's easy. It's easy to be in the moment. That's why one afternoon lasted a thousand years. Now, you've been socialised and edu-ma-cationalised and you're always thinking about the next thing; now it takes something special to switch your mind back on and turn your brain off. Folks do find ways though. What better way than to lose yourself in the roll of the wheels, the harmony of riding? It doesn't have to be dangerous, heck it doesn't have to be cool and it sure as @#$% doesn't need to be no transcendental hippy guru nonsense. It's all about you, coming face to face with the holy moment, once in a while, because you need it more than anything else in your messy, fucked up modern life.

# South Korean flow

When I get on my bike and clip into my pedals, it's like hitting a big red launch button. I get on, I start to roll, and the world around me is reduced to a blur. I spin up, zone into the flow of traffic, and all but the asphalt dematerializes into vapor trails and dust clouds.

Vapor trails, dust clouds, inconsolable car horns, vacuous pedestrians, apoplectic taxi drivers, slaughterous buses, impossible scooters with delivery boxes on the back, incomprehensible scooters with tragically pretty and suspiciously young prostitutes on the back, dogs with ears and tails dyed purple and pink, baby carriages filled with trash pickings, delivery trucks with Hite and soju, teenage girls watching Big Bang music videos on their cell phones, middle aged men watching teenage girls watching music videos on their cell phones, little kids with young mothers glaring at the middle aged men, and all of them vying with one another for unoccupied space on their way from one place to another at unreasonable speed and none of them giving a shit that the concept of right of way does not exist in South Korea.

It comes down to flow. Flow that may or may not exist, depending on how you look at it. I came here with American traffic in my head, attempted to hit the launch button on the second day, and quickly found myself jumping a curb onto the sidewalk to avoid a frenzied mass of something I clearly didn't understand well enough to navigate effectively. I couldn't even see the flow, let alone work with it. As far as I was concerned when I got here, there was no sense or shape to any of it. I have since come to see it. I have since come to understand it. I have since come to go with it, play in it, and even (at certain select times) help sculpt it into something even more liquid and interesting.

When I hit that launch button, I go like a bottle rocket that never burns out, never explodes, never fades out. Never fades out except when the feeling of massive steel pistons leaves my legs and is replaced with a sensation of being powered by an unfortunate arrangement of cracked wooden dowel rods and dried out rubber bands. My breathing becomes heavy, legs heavier still, and I begin to wonder if my tires are going flat. I drift out to shallower, slower waters and let everything to my immediate left become a bit more distant and less relevant. Rest or food or both are in order. That big red button taps into reserves that become depleted and I too-often nearly run them dry.

When the reserves run low, others might shift into a lower gear or coast for a while until the speed runs out. I don't. I can't. I'm not interested. One gear, no coasting, the fixed gear bicycle is a fixed idea that requires one to acknowledge the variability of the physical and mental self. There are no excuses, no illusions on this bike. Even the brake is simply a small insurance policy against the fallout from one's inevitable failure to react in time. A way to go and a way to stop in the same simple mechanism, and a little help with the latter function if need be. That's all one needs, and I appreciate it for the fact that it does not complicate an already complicated situation. With as many things around me that I need to account for as I have, the simplest, most reliable machine possible is what I want under me. After all, the greater the complexity of the tool of navigation, the more likely it is it may interfere, and the last thing I want is to lose touch with the flow.

*David R. Munson, South Korea*

## Nirvana is just a bike ride away

I heard someone say: 'You know this thing about Zen is just crap, the main thing you feel on a Fixie is scared'. I had to interrupt. Zen is about bypassing or exhausting the emotions and the rational mind to directly experience reality in all its terrifying, naked glory. Fear is a perfectly sensible reaction to Zen, just as it is a sensible reaction to the possibility of imminent mangling by a vehicle. You might think you can't reach enlightenment by riding fixed but it's no more or less crazy a method than meditating without sleep for days on end while some lunatic beats you periodically with a stick. Try it! That could be a genuine 'First'. Picture the headline . . . Cyclist attains State of Enlightenment During SF Alley Cat.

## RESPECT TO ALL THOSE THAT MADE THIS BOOK POSSIBLE:

Riders, contributors, photographers, forums, crews and above all riders everywhere. Chapeau!

p1 Brenton Salo / p3 Iacopo Boccalari / p4 Gavin Strange / p6 Yasin Rahim / p8 Gary Shove / p10 Yasin Rahim/ p11-p12 Yasin Rahim / p13 Tristan Wheelock / p14 Yasin Rahim / p16 Tristan Wheelock / p19 Tristan Wheelock / p20 Tristan Wheelock / p22 Thomas Olson / p23 Thomas Olson / p24 Thomas Olson / p25 Thomas Olson / p25 Thomas Olson / p26 Jeff Luger / p28 Alistair Reid / p29 Brenton Salo / p30-p35 photo-goooove, assistant-ruitek / p36 Chris Willmore / p37 photo-goooove, assistant-ruitek / p38 Jeff Luger / p40 Tristan Wheelock / p43-p45 Jordi Tamayo and Cristian Marin / p46 Yasin Rahim / p48 Gaetan Rossier / p50 Jordi Tamayo and Cristian Marin / p51 Gaetan Rossier / p52 Cyril Saulnier / p53 Cyril Saulnier / p54 Haiqal Anwar / p55 Dennis Lo / p56 Tristan Wheelock / p58 Yasin Rahim / p59 Yasin Rahim / p60 Yasin Rahim / p61 Yasin Rahim / p62 Jason Rosete / p64 Jason Rosete / p65 Jason Rosete / p67 Mathieu Prentout / p68 Mathieu Prentout / p69 Jason Rosete / p70 Mathieu Prentout / p71 Komet, Kristian Hallberg / p72 Alistair Reid / p73 Yasin Rahim / p74 Jeff Luger / p75 Jeff Luger / p76 photo-goooove, assistant-ruitek / p77 Dennis Lo / p80 Tristan Wheelock / p82 Jordi Tamayo and Cristian Marin / p83 Jordi Tamayo and Cristian Marin / p84 Chris Willmore, Mathieu Prentout, all others photo-goooove, assistant-ruitek / p86 Mathieu Prentout / p88-97 Adam Scott / p98 Tristan Wheelock / p100 Yasin Rahim / p102 Dennis Lo / p103 Dennis Lo / p104-p105 Yasin Rahim / p106 Jeff Luger / p107 Jason Rosete / p108-p112 Jordi Tamayo and Cristian Marin / p113 Haiqal Anwar / p114-p115 Jordi Tamayo and Cristian Marin / p116 David Munson / p117 Jeff Luger / p118 Jordi Tamayo and Cristian Marin / p119 Chris Willmore / p120-p122 Gary Shove / p124 Haiqal Anwar / p125-128 Gary Shove / p130 Dennis Lo / p131 Chris Willmore / p132 Yasin Rahim / p133 David Munson / p134 Brenton Salo / p136 Jason Rosete / p140-p145 Jason Rosete / p148-p149 Alan Sikiric / p151

Nicholas Firan, photo-goooove, assistant-ruitek / p152-p153 Yasin Rahim / p154 Dennis Lo / p156 Danilo Zigenbard / p157 Yasin Rahim / p158 Brenton Salo / p159 photo-goooove, assistant-ruitek / p161 Jordi Tamayo and Cristian Marin / p162 Brenton Salo / p165 Chris Willmore / p166-p169 Yasin Rahim / p170 Riki Taniuchi / p172 Richard Heneghan / p173 Iacopo Boccalari / p175-p177 Jeff Luger / p179 Chris Willmore / p180 Khaled Ben-Rabha / p181 Phil Thomas / p182 Brenton Salo / p183 Chris Willmore / p185 Riki Taniuchi / p186 Gianfranco Tripodo / p188 Tristan Wheelock / p189 Yasin Rahim, Enciclika, Brenton Salo, PhilipThomas, CAS, Dennis Lo / p190 Tristan Wheelock / p192 David Munson

## SPECIAL THANKS TO:

Mr 36, Tristan, Jason, Alan, Chris, Jordi, Cristian, Dennis, Condition NYC, Gilagila, Chris, Adam, Riki, Yasin, David, Jeff, Patrick, Phil, Khaled, Gaetan, Thomas, Mathieu, Nabiis, Thomas, Macaframa, Gianfranco, Eisuke, CAS, Enciclika

## DISCLAIMER:

None of the words and spaces contained herein have any relevance to any of the photographs. They are only included to keep the pictures company.

All images are copyright of their respective owner.

## RESPECT COPYRIGHT:

COLLABORATE AND CREATE. All images submitted by contributors have been supplied on the understanding that they as originator retain copyright and are credited.

Additional commentary by riders, photographers from around the globe plus other famous people.

Back Page Images: Jordi Tamayo and Cristian Marin / Anton Volger.

**Crank Arm Steady**

**In the darkness, I hurt myself...**

The young brave takes the tomahawk and cuts off his own little finger. Somewhere something dies and something is born. There are many roads to heaven and all of them are hidden. What is beautiful is not good, what is good is not beautiful. When the world is upside down, you climb on the ceiling just to get your head straight. Somewhere someone cuts their own skin, someone changes the channel and scratches their ass, someone bombs down a hill in heavy traffic on a skinny frame and two knife thin wheels. Whatever you say brave, the cult of death is as old as time. The ones who survive their walk in the desert, know what life is worth. They're the only ones to trust. Everyone else is sleepwalking.